Railman's Son

poems by

LeRoy N. Sorenson

Finishing Line Press
Georgetown, Kentucky

Railman's Son

ACKNOWLEDGMENTS

The following poems (or versions of these poems) have appeared in the following
journals:

An Anvil Has Fallen, *American Journal of Poetry*, Volume 5, 2018.
The Boy, *Comstock Review*, Spring/Summer, 2019.
Getting Over It, *Collateral Damage: A Pirene's Fountain Anthology*, 2018.
In a Black Year, *Naugatuck River Review*, 2017.
The Junk Kid, *American Journal of Poetry*, Volume 5, 2018.
Roundhouse Remembrance, *The Cape Rock,* Issue Forty-Five, Number 2, 2017.
She Hated Clutter, *The Sow's Ear Poetry Review*, Volume XXVIII, No.2, Summer
        2018.
Spying on My Father Watching Pro Wrestling, *Comstock Review*, Volume 34:1, Spring
        Summer, 2020.
Tarred Roofs in Huron, South Dakota, *riverSedge: A Journal of Art and Literature*,
        Volume 32, Issue 1.
The Tear Down, *Broad River Review*, July 2018.
The Tilting Saddle Bar, *Crab Orchard Review, Ka-Ching: The Money Issue*, Volume
        23.3, March 2019.
Tomato Soup Reminds Me of Poverty, *The Tishman Review*
Train Wreck 1958, *The Cider Press Review*, Volume 18.1, 2016.

Publisher: Leah Huete de Maines
Editor: Christen Kincaid
Cover Art: Dreamstime
Author Photo: Hakan Carlsson
Cover Design: Elizabeth Maines McCleavy

Printed in the USA on acid-free paper.
Order online: www.finishinglinepress.com
        also available on amazon.com

Author inquiries and mail orders:
Finishing Line Press
P. O. Box 1626
Georgetown, Kentucky 40324
U. S. A.

Table of Contents

To my best friends:
David Feroe, Jeff Nicholson and Chris Sullivan

She Hated Clutter

She folded my dead father's army uniform,
folded it into a cedar chest she never opened.
Threw away sweaters, bras, panties.
Donated armchairs, pillows, sheets.
But she kept the Bibles—even the ones
in German—and every time I returned

home, the house seemed thinner, the small
rooms more barren, each step an echo.
When a child, I dreamt again and again
about being shuttled from one orphanage
to another. Before her death, I returned

once again and found her throwing photo
albums into a large garbage can. *You don't
need this stuff.* Photos of my grandparents,
great-grandparents. Photos of cousins I never
knew, photos of my sister and me. I woke
up cold that night, ready for her death,

ready to become an orphan. I sat in that tiny
kitchen, a photo album opened to a picture
of a boy, armed for survival, gun belt wrapped
around his hips, two toy pistols aimed at the camera.

Tomato Soup Reminds Me of Poverty

That was the summer my mother slouched
at the table, so beaten down, numbed
by the death of her first son burnt deep
into her bones while my father sat
at table's end, working into a fury.
The summer I flailed at curve balls,
beat up once a week by the Schmidt
brothers. I walked the railroad yards
between steaming engines
and peeling, off-red boxcars.
Every day the wind blew
in from the southeast where the meat
plant sat, the stench of shit and blood.
I walked on Main, sneaking glances
into the faces of those escapees
from the bars; those ruined
faces, those tired faces looted
of hope. Their bunched shoulders.
Waiting for me, a cracked
linoleum floor, another bowl
of tomato soup and my father
in another rage. The summer
my mother first crossed her hands
and wept. The summer I vowed
never to return. The summer I prayed
for amnesty. The summer when each
day dripped into a soiled
twilight and the wind shifted—clean
and cool from the north.

Being American:

The streets, you know, are full of danger:
cars run red lights, wild walkers
in banter about the best rifles
and second mortgages. This is where
you learned to speak the shorthand
of American rage: *fuckhead, asshole,
get out of my way.* Anyone can hurt
you at any time. This week a man,
wearing a baseball cap, throws
bricks into the faces of passing bike
riders. White men, with assault rifles,
patrol a southern Black neighborhood.

Of course, there is work. Not enough.
Right-wing think tanks assure that other
jobs (non-union) will spring like snakes
from the forehead of American Capitalism.
For Tyrone with bent fingers. For Susan
with aching back, fallen arches.
Conservatives blame the *Immigration
Problem.* You can ride a Greyhound
west or south. But, if you leave, you return
home only for funerals. You learn
more American—*geographic mobility,
shrinking working class* or *retraining.*
In any gin joint, you stand in front
of a mirror, in the dark, to imagine any face
but your own.

Manufactured, stamped, outsourced.
You trek to find that job that
pays more than your grandfather earned.
Sometimes you think things can't get worse,
then they do. Your son needs special ed;
the schools offer none. You need
hernia surgery but there is no money.
Or maybe you put your hope
into the Lottery or a bouncing red ball.
The odds no worse than those you already face.

Foundries gone; assembly lines robot
run. You are left with stacking boxes
in a warehouse, a grin that broadcasts
stubbornness, feet firmly planted
for the next brawl. And a second job
cleaning floors and toilets in a bar.
Some politician announces:
Americans need to work more.
You labor sixty hours a week
and are forty-five, with a bent
spine. Your body no longer
a temple. To anything.

The Junk Kid

Manny Jackson, the toughest kid on the block,
stands on the playground, feet planted wide,
ready to teach someone, anyone, a lesson.
His head leans out of his dingy blue jacket
like a turtle. And if I told you he just got
beaten that morning by his drunk father;

switched across the back of his bony legs,
blood spitting on his feet, you might shake
your head. His home reeks of burnt
onions, sweat and desolation. He sleeps
with two brothers, one who, most nights,
pisses the bed. He has trouble inhaling

because of his broken nose, broken by a raging
father. And if I told you his mother stands
on a street corner, lost, unable to cross
because devils lurk in the grocery store
or hide out in the bathroom behind the closed door,
the door with peeling yellow paint, you might shake

your head again, more slowly. Her preacher man
looks down on Manny and tells him he deserves
what he gets. You don't want to stand
too close to him in baseball warmups.
He's got a sour smell about him, sometimes
has head lice. He often cries in the bathroom

at school. Manny is a junk kid in a junk school.
I once heard him singing in that run-down
Baptist Church off Main. Singing with a voice
so pure my heart ached. What if I told you I saw
him on his knees on Percy boulevard

holding a dead yellow cat, weeping, fist
flaying the air, looking for anyone
to blame. He goes to Nam, loses one leg.
What if told you, afterwards, his left hand
shivers so much he can't hold a fork.

What if I told you that I will never enter
a kitchen smelling of fried onions,
and not remember Manny, that junk
kid, and think I love him like I love
my brother. I love him. What if I told you that.

Tarred Roofs in Huron, South Dakota

I worked labor jobs that summer,
worked construction on ground
soaked with rotgut and beer. Worked
on the ashen remains of an old saloon.
Worked next to the James, willows
lining its banks, brown sluggish
water drifting south. On its banks,

the Baptist minister and Mrs. T. killed
themselves, together, sitting under
the drooping trees. The foreman
a lapsed Communist who found
the Light at the Jesus Saves
Temple near the graveyard.
Before work, he told good stories,

Tales about gun fights with Revenuers
and liquor runs to Chicago.
He'd say: *Watch your asses, boys.*
Never thought I'd do this shit
for thirty years. Each day, the sky
grew white under a savage sun.
I carried 50-pound cement bags

from delivery trucks to foundation
trenches dug in rock-dry soil.
I hated cement dust as it sifted
into my clothes, stuck onto my skin.
I wore sunglasses and bandanas, red,
to keep cement swirl from eyes
and nostrils. The bags too heavy

for my 130-pound frame.
Every day the same grind—
lift, carry, dump. By noon, I stripped
off my shirt, burned the acne off
my back. Forearms scabbed as I labored
in a drought-wasted summer.

The foreman felt cheated; his youth spent
in troop carriers and Korean winters.
He'd shout get *your asses in gear,*
you bastards. He often sat on a stump,

head slumped, hands over his eyes
and I heard him pray. The crew
often hungover and snarly. *Motherfucker*
their favorite curse. Billy and Art and fat Sam.

fellow crewmen. They spent their nights
in Hurst's' bar, told lies about their brave
deeds and the pussy they got in Chicago.
Each day they woke hung over. Short
tempered. Jammed skinny legs into blue
jeans, feet into scuffed construction boots,
ready for a battle that never came. My last

job tarring flat roofs, grading black goo
into a smooth surface. Even with gloves,
my hands turned sooty black. The tar
stunk, numbing my nostrils. Every deep
inhale tasted like vomit. Our sweat
evaporated under the sky's fire.

At day's end, I ate with my parents,
prowled empty, darkened streets, sought
counsel from a half-moon. In a dream
that night, I find my way to the river, swim
across to stumble upon row after row
of faded barns, their doors barely hanging
on rusted hinges. Ghost winds
inhabit them. Above me, the stars,
orphan spirits like my own.

In a Black Year

The fisherman hangs his line
into a river three inches deep.
In a bucket next to his waders,
fish, none the size of a meal.
It is the year of drought, no job,
no money; his days a blur.
Even the old guys
have given up—no fish, no water.
Above, a yellow orb of torture;
his torso sweat drenched, ahead
a long trek to home across rail tracks
through a burned-out park, soil
like poured concrete.

He hates the betrayed look
in his wife's green eyes, cannot look
his kids in the eye. He hates
the men still working, the men
bringing home a paycheck,
the men still laughing at crude jokes.
He has lost his sense of time.
He is living in the wrong town
in the wrong country. Men tell
him to go north for work.

And so go his days: he forgets
his address, churches beam false
hope. He remembers the comfort
of Sunday sermons, organ music
that astonished him. The rhythm
of a crew of men, shovels in hand,
digging up overturned box cars.
Tuesday night dominoes in Pete's tavern.

All gone now. What's left are midnights
at the kitchen table, unable to sleep,
unable to cry for help. He endures.
He aches for his hands wrapped around
a pickaxe, grease ground into his palms,
craves a job, any job.

There is nothing so pure as work.

Train Wreck, 1958

My father stirs in the kitchen, boiling coffee,
crisping fried potatoes, night sleep a seldom
companion. The sun pale through the windows.
He's headed east on a train, wears bib
overalls, heavy black shoes. He readies
a lunch pail for a white bread sandwich
and a steel thermos for coffee.

Through Brookings and farther east,
the train presses forward, railmen stuffed
into a caboose. Big Henry can't shut
up, piling lie upon lie about Chicago
nights and all the women he had.
Eddy leans his elbows on his thighs,
covers his broad face with splayed hands,
queasy from tremors and shakes.

Most of the men have shaved heads
and bent fingers from slamming boxcar
doors. Many flash to train rides
in WW II, their frigid hands, cold sweat
fouling the air. Sol's cousin shredded
by a mortar; my father's brother shot
in the chest. He survived.

The men head to a derailed train, ready to dig,
pull crossbars from debris—frozen mud
everywhere. Rail cars burn, black plumes
blotting the sun. The men mine twisted rails,
digging them out from under overturned
boxcars, flinch from the wail of metal

on metal. The danger of smashed hands,
severed legs in the front of their minds.
But you get paid time-and-a-half—some extra
money for Xmas or a round of booze
at that rotgut bar near the roundhouse.
The men pray, mostly, or swear,
the danger an intoxication, a release.
When done, they return west, slog
home covered in mud.

My father, that night, sits in a wooden
kitchen chair, shoulders stooped,
trying to remember something good—
not the whistles of mortars, not shards
of ashes falling from burning boxcars.
Outside, the western sky a starless void.

He studies his hands, grimed ashen,
and eats his bread, carefully, one slice
at a time, sopping up the gravy
until a blank plate remains.

Taken

Two blocks from the rail yard
stood a saloon built like a shotgun—
tables on one wall and a battered oak
bar on the other. The Sanders twins, Sally
and Lenore, stayed on as barmaids
for years, sisters with black walnut
hair and a taut bounce of sex
and nerve. Their brown eyes stared,

never wavered as the men checked
them out. Young railmen, hog
butchers slouched into horseshoes,
slumped over Johnny Walker shots
and cold drafts of Pabst or Schmidt.
Most Thursday nights, Levi Waldner held
court with tales of his long trips on rail
cars and tramp steamers—Shanghai,
Manilla, New Orleans—cities

of intrigue, alluring women, haze
and fog the taste of them. He roamed
after the War, roamed with his head
swiveled over his shoulder, roamed
with his night tremors just hours away.

He never left the prison camp behind him,
never mentioned month-long bouts
in his one room walk-up, too fearful to open
his door, walk down the street.

Dread flooded his pale eyes, drove
his voice higher and louder,
his right index finger stabbed cigarette
vapor with every word. Neon lights
tainted the listeners green red blue.

Levi always closed down the bar, opened
the back door; the whispered voices
of his next nightmare spilled into the exposed
night; his exhaustion so deep
even dying seemed like wasted effort.

She Goes for a Walk

Each year, she walks on the first
snow to the graveyard at the south
end, near the river. Its crunch feels
just right under her boots. The road bright
silver under the street lamps.
The night still. Tiny houses dark,
houses with small panes of glass, hold
the night close. Her child was born
in a snow month. She knows where
the grave is, even in the snow,
even at night. There are no flowers
in the winter, just polished granite.
Cold. Bare. She wipes the flat
marker clean, stands over it.
Stands as the snow swirls, stands
with her head bowed. She wants
to go farther out into the prairie,
but she knows she will turn
back into town, moon and stars
casting her body into a long,
solitary shadow.

The Boy

The father plods from funeral to gravesite
back to his black Buick and sits.

                              Revs the motor,
smoking the tenth Camel of the day.

His black suit too small for his shoulders.
Once home, the father chops up

                              all the Bibles,

and pisses on them before he pours
gasoline on the mess and lights it.

He is a man at war,

                              How the flames
singe his fingers, blister them for days.

Later, he will be surprised by his wife's anger,
his mother's anguished words. But he damn well

knows he did the right thing. He can still feel
                                        the grasp

of his tiny fingers. His son dead.
                              Two months old.

Heritage

I wasn't the handiest of boys. Hammers,
chisels, crosscut saws gave me fits, refused
to bend to my intent. After college, I worked

in a Malt-o-Meal factory, standing at the end
of a conveyor belt waiting for large plastic
bags to pack into a cardboard boxes, thirty

to a box. My back became an aching arc,
my hands sliced by cardboard. Breaks lasted
ten minutes, twice a night. The air reeked

with a sweet burn. They put me at the end
so I couldn't screw up something more important—
bearings, exhaust fans, the conveyor belt.

I remember how, when a boy, my father
dragged me up with him to reshingle
our roof; to rip out tear and rot

until nothing remained but plywood. I used
the claw end of a hammer, slipping and sliding
on the roof's slant. I once loved

watching my father, shovel in his muddy hands, dig
holes for fence posts in our backyard. He never did
anything easy. Later, I stayed away from him

and constant chores, stayed away from the bars
he once took me to but, much later, found my own.
Found myself in an empty bed, shivering,

beer bottles in a neat row on the bedside table.
And I think of that last summer home—
my father and his hammers and nails, his shovels

and fence posts, his hands grimy from railyard
oil. Silent drives to this lumber yard or that hardware

store. And how angry I was about how he ignored
me, his son so unlike him. And how I hated his tools.

That summer, a drunk cousin—his favorite nephew—
drove him in a pickup to the pool hall or Elmer's Corner.

They belly laughed, told tales, my father's arm around
his shoulder. How absurd I was, so jealous, so

unforgiving. I spouted politics he despised.
How I ridiculed his beliefs, looked down on his job.

How, intentionally, I lost my last chance for his love.

Spying on My Father Watching Pro Wrestling

That man, Baron von Raschke, a helluva of a wrestler.
My father paused, out of breath. *And that Claw move;*
best damn thing I've ever seen. In the living room
on Friday nights, he sat in his chair, a recliner, glued
to those AWA matches with the Crusher,
the Barbarian, the Warlord. His wife in bed again; no
goodnight, no peck on the lips. Home from a ten
hour day, he twisted and turned in front of the black
and white replaying this blow or that one.

I don't know how he did it, work that is.
Bad back, bad knee, the old war wound aching
year round. Soaked his hands in the kitchen sink
to rub out grease and dirt, scraping his fingernails
on a bar of Ivory to remove tar. A losing battle
like everything else. He loved those tough guys;
the world he knew crumbling in growl. Some nights,
I climbed from my bed and witnessed him perched
on the edge of his chair, head bowed, hands cupped
over his nearly shaved scalp. His face gray stubble.

By day, he labored in a roundhouse, week
after week, no end in sight. Maybe I was too young,
maybe too afraid, I never gripped
his shoulders, never told him of my love.
Years later, I understood: he was born
to work, knew he would die without work.
In front of that black and white, he'd play
out his Golden Glove days, the breathless joy
and pain of them. Bunch his shoulders, ready
for fight—any fight that, once again, made
him feel just a little bit alive.

Roundhouse Remembrance

Before oil and grit sandpaper my throat,
before howl pares down everything
to nothing, I go back to the roundhouse
where my father spent his days;
go back to hear Jim still boss
Fat Jerry and Elmer to this task
or that. Return to a hollow cavern,
to steam and clangs and squeals.
I go back to the fire in my father's eyes
because I burn in my blood in the way
he did and I must walk the line, just
as he did, from my hometown
to Brookings and Prior Lake
and Waseca and New Ulm.
I need to see those railmen,
clothes oil-streaked, wipe
their shiny faces with grimy
red bandanas, gather around
a stalled steam engine, take
turns with crowbars to beat
the stuck pistons. I have to climb
this shaky ladder with my father
to the roof of the depot and survey
the naked sky as he holds
my hand, as he never did,
tousles my hair, as he never did,
and sing in the voice of those men
before my song turns sour.

The Way Is Lost

This morning may be brilliant;
sunlight filters through and my shadow,
a long curious beast, stretches
to the west across rows of graves.
Year after year, I forget where the plots

are even though the headstones stand
sentinel and the same paved trails
snake through green nubs of prairie grass.
Below the roots, old Bibles, decayed
shoes, gray tweeds and simple A-lines.

It's important to look good before the casket
closes. Off to one side, a fresh grave dug,
a coffin laid, peonies and roses
strewn. I can almost hear the wails
and hymns. I walk with small wary

steps, unsure of the way, walk
toward a ravine where the sun fails
to warm, where my dead reside.
Buried with them, the memories
of bars painted with stench,

howls for their dead babies, the sudden
need to dance even in black debris.
I am old with this grief, tired of its yoke.

The Teardown

A man stumbles out of his car,
sunglasses in one hand, ready
to fight off the wind. He surveys
brown fields, bends into the wind
as if bowing before an altar.

The sky a blur of washed blue.
He steps onto gravel, studies an
abandoned tractor, its seat rusted;
a tractor like the one he sat
on as a boy. There is nothing left
of the house, the artesian well,
the barn. Everything torn down

for more crops. His hands still itch
from the stiff wool of a lamb's head;
his tongue still savors the onion-filled
hamburgers of his youth. A ten-building
town a half mile away. The town
with a shotgun country joint, gleaming
oak bar. The town where he learned pool

on tiptoes. The bar where he began
to learn the language of men:
the grunts, the turn-of-the-knife insults,
the endless will to humiliate and win.
An abandoned mortuary sat a few doors
down, a rotted place where William and Mary
and Anne, his grandmother's children,

all lay before the age of five. He thinks
about a grandfather he never knew buried
a hundred miles away and his aunt
shriveled with longing for the return
of her dead fiancé. His mother
and her dead son. This is the farm
where he learned the never-ending
price of love. These memories
razor-sharp in his throat.

No Exit

Just outside Tracy, a pickup with rusted fenders
and a grey metallic finish stopped and I climbed
in a cab filled with smoke and a red headed woman—
the skin on her left arm burned pink, freckles
highlighted in the sun. I said Huron and she nodded,
dragged on the butt in her right hand, slammed
the gear shift through its paces. She straddled

the pickup over the lane divider; we peeled
the road asunder one mile at a time. She glanced
at me, her green eyes wide. *If we keep going
straight,* she said, *first the Rockies then the Pacific,*
nodded to the radio, a Waylon Jennings baritone
about lost lovers. *Sex,* she said. *It's the only thing
keeping us going.* Instead, we went through one

nameless town after another, waving wheat and green
corn sentinels, drove on the edge of a ditch
a few feet from the tire rims edge. A few feet
from oblivion. When she glanced again, I turned shy,
imagined my face red. Next on the radio an early
Willie Nelson. She told me about her dead boy,

her dead husband; she chain smoked, her left hand
gripping the steering wheel. She still wore a ring,
a thin gold ribbon sliding back and forth on her finger.
I remember when she drove away, a sudden
horn salute a pitcher's toss from where I stood
and I wanted, again, the tart smell of her. She drove
west, the sun almost gone—west to the Pacific;
west, to a place where blue never ends.

I knew loss, but I had no understanding
of an ache so deep in my throat that pain
was the only sound I spoke: I remember
how I put my hand on her taut shoulder
as we drove to Huron, the town dust
dry, my hand cramping; how we rode
in silence, radio off, my youth no comfort.

You Can Return

and see again the shy boy even the pimply
girls ignored. The math teacher
with the broken garter dangled just below

temptation. Relive your cousin's toss
of a black horseshoe into the bluest sky.
Suppose you were nothing but a shadow?

Suppose you were responsible for the wet
pallor of your mother's brow, had only a dirty
hand to wipe it dry? Remember the baseball

bat you had when ten. How you loved
the smooth gleam of its wood, its generous crack
when a fastball was hit just so. You loved

playing under a sky that had no regrets,
its purpose clear by just being.
You believed in a love so burning.

And a neighbor girl with nerve.
Suppose you have a heart plundered
with despair and that's why these blues

always beckon, especially if you are a romantic
tramp, especially if the rattle of your bones
becomes a hymn.

And if these blues
never go away. What then?

Almost Everything

You cut your engine on the gravel road
and wait for the dust to settle. Your parents,
grandparents, uncles and aunts stretched
across two graveyards in patches
and solitary headstones. You have breakfast,
that morning, with a cousin mad for god.

You are his earth, his vessel, your very skin
of his choosing. You don't believe.
Here's what happens: one day
you kneel over the graves of your parents,
trace their names and relive the constant
anger of one and the grief of the other,
each chained to their dead baby.

A baby with his skull crushed
in childbirth by forceps. You return
to your motel, study the mini bar, ignore
prints of ducks and pheasants. You open
the curtain window. Outside a black
parking lot, pickaxed prairie
and a northwest gale, the vessel

that sweeps everything pure.
Then imagine your mother sang
my blued-eyed boy as she stooped
to lift your brother, gasped
as she saw his crushed skull, gasped
as she glimpsed a blue sky seen
through his skull. Survive—
that was the first lesson you learned.

The Tilting Saddle Bar
(after James Wright)

Down the splintered steps, I turn
toward the James and its steep banks
strangled with cattails and hobo weeds.
Upstream, at the Third Street bridge,
looms the Hormel plant, its whistle
wailing and its doors opening to the early
evening crickets. The men pour down
the long hill, pour down to the river
and over the bridge into a pale sun,
past abandoned railcars into silo
shadows and beckoning downtown lights.
With abandon, I run through the river park
to catch them—then straggle behind
as some head to shanty houses;
others to neon. And I trail them.
Downtown, one old man, face purple
stands near a bar door that swings on tight
hinges and glares at the men then me.
And I plunge in and find scrawny
women, faces uplifted, legs crossed.
In the back, sit laid-off railmen—
my father one—three drinks into the night.
His eyes blurry, his voice loud over the jukebox.
I cringe. Patrons, now sloppy drunk,
pinching women's asses as they head
to the can. The air sweat filled, smoke tinged.
More whiskey shots and beer chasers.
The men's faces drunk red, their eyes
shining with coming madness.
Then the shadow boxing, the boasts,
some guy puking in the corner. Two guys
pick him up, put him on a bar stool, order
him two whiskeys. They laugh when his hands
shake too much to hold a shot glass.
My stomach roils and my father shouts: Son.
And the stale beer and the cigarettes
sink into my pores for all
the coming years of my life.

An Anvil Has Fallen

Henry grabbed his mug, broken
pinky sticking out at an odd
angle. A perfect forecaster
of rain and snow and ice.

His spine hurts like hell. Injured
when a bunch of pipes rolled off
a flat car, knocked him on his back,
the stony ground ripping his skin.

He holds his stein in his left hand—
his right hand shakes too much. His doctor
says lead poison. The factory
bosses deny everything. No one

stands with him. The union busted
years ago. His back hurts so much
he bites his lip so he won't sob
in public. He feels wound up.

Angry most of the time, he wants
to slug anyone near him but his hand
shakes and he can't punch straight.
He never thought his life

would turn out this way. Pain pills.
Straight shots with beer chasers
sitting at a cracked bartop at noon.
Trying to blank out the day, trying

to stay numb. He slides off the stool,
returns to the machine shop. Broken legs.
Mangled hands. Anyone who works the floor
knows the price. At the end of shift,

the foreman shouts: *Load 'em up.*
The men scramble for a trolley, dump
foot-wide pipes onto them, pull
them to the waiting flatbeds,

flatbeds scorched black
One guy spits on the pipes,
polishes them with his sleeve.
Not even a hint on the curved

surfaces of the men who labored
to make the once grainy surfaces smooth.

Getting Over It

I've never gotten over northwest gales,
the reds and yellows of tulips, the paradise

of fall wheat. I have never gotten
over brother, parents, grandparents, aunts

and uncles, cousins and lovers dead
before I was forty. The stinging smell

of a woman's wet hair intrigues
me as does my best friend's search

to find the prime well of truth.
I don't believe in the clean break

from misery. I believe in regret, the stain
of history. I believe in shaking trees,

air sick and forlorn. I believe in the treason
of the heart. And my heart cleaved.

And the evil of the descending belt.

I believe in a language stripped
of all words but ache.

Homework

(after Rebecca McClanahan)

Needing them still, I come
when I can, this time to the old house
where we once shared
six little rooms; mine a closet
bedroom glued to the front.
The house where my father raged,
raged at me, raged at his life
and at my mother cowed on a broken
couch, her eyes hazel slate.
I studied hours into the night,
alone, so I could escape,
just my father's snores
for company. My father seemed
a giant then; my mother someone
to protect. There were the days
she lay in bed, one son
already dead. There were the nights
my father dragged
me to this pool hall or that bar.
How easy to be so alone
in such a tiny place. How I, now,
listen to the silence that has never
left me, aching for a life
other than the one I had.

How little there was.

LeRoy N. Sorenson was born and raised in Huron, South Dakota. During his youth and teen years, the town was a railroad, meat packing and grain hauling town – a mini-Pittsburgh on the prairie. His father was a railman and his mother a hotel maid. In his senior year, he won a National Council of Teachers Award which allowed him to go to college. He attended St. Olaf College in Minnesota and participated in an experimental college-within-a-college called Paracollege. He majored in childhood intellectual development. After college, he worked as a child counselor, political organizer, and research associate. He completed post-graduate studies in anthropology and economics at the University of Minnesota in Economics, focusing on Third World economic development, public finance and statistics. He then entered and graduated from the MBA program at the University of Minnesota.

After graduating, Mr. Sorenson took a job at a small Minneapolis investment banking firm and became a Certified Financial Analyst. He worked at that firm for thirty years writing investment reports on firms and projects and designing investment opportunities for pension funds, insurance companies and institutional money managers.

Mr. Sorenson returned to writing at the Loft Literary Center in Minneapolis. The Loft chose him as a poetry participant in its Mentor and Foreword programs. Main Street Rag published Mr. Sorenson's debut poetry collection, *Forty Miles North of Nowhere*. He has won The Tishman Review 2019 Edna St. Vincent Millay Prize for Poetry. He was a finalist in Naugatuck River Review's annual poetry contest and a semifinalist in the *Nimrod International Journal of Prose and Poetry*'s Pablo Neruda Prize in Poetry. His work has appeared or will appear in *The American Journal of Poetry, the Atlanta Review, the Baltimore Review, The Cider Press Review, Crab Orchard Review, Comstock Review, The Sow's Ear Poetry Review* and other journals. He lives in St. Paul, MN with his wife, a novelist.

CPSIA information can be obtained
at www.ICGtesting.com
Printed in the USA
JSHW042114230321
12803JS00001BA/45

9 781646 624515